ISBN: 9781763833838

First Edition

For every Esmeralda.
May you always feel *elated*.

Pippa Bird
Elated Emu

In the warm glow of morning light,
Esmeralda the Emu felt something bright.

She pranced through the bush, feathered and free,
Seeking the word for her mysterious glee.

First came Quincy Quokka with a munch,
'Emotional, perhaps?' He offered a hunch.

Esmeralda asked, 'What does emotional mean?'
Quincy explained, 'Strong feelings unseen.'

Esmeralda smiled, but continued her quest,
For the perfect word to describe her zest.

Kiya Koala in the eucalyptus high,
'Ecstatic,' she said with a sleepy sigh.

Esmeralda inquired, 'What's ecstatic, Kiya?'
The koala replied, 'Joy, like the sky's on fire.'

Esmeralda thanked her, yet still she trod,
In search of the word that felt like a nod.

Frank the Frilled-neck basking in the sand,
Suggested 'euphoric,' with a flick of his hand.

Esmeralda asked, 'What does euphoric mean?'
Frank explained, 'An intense joy, like a dream.'

But Esmeralda knew it wasn't quite right,
And kept on her path, so airy and light.

Penelope Platypus in the creek's cool flow,
Thought 'exhilarated' might be the glow.

Esmeralda wondered, 'What does exhilarated mean, Penelope?'
The platypus said, 'Thrilled, like a splash in the stream's melody.'

Esmeralda considered, but shook her head,
For the word she sought was still unsaid.

Then came Kirri Kangaroo with a bounce in her gait,
'Elated!' She declared, and Esmeralda felt great.

'What's elated?' Esmeralda asked with pending glee,
Calm Kangaroo replied, 'It's joy, pure and free.'

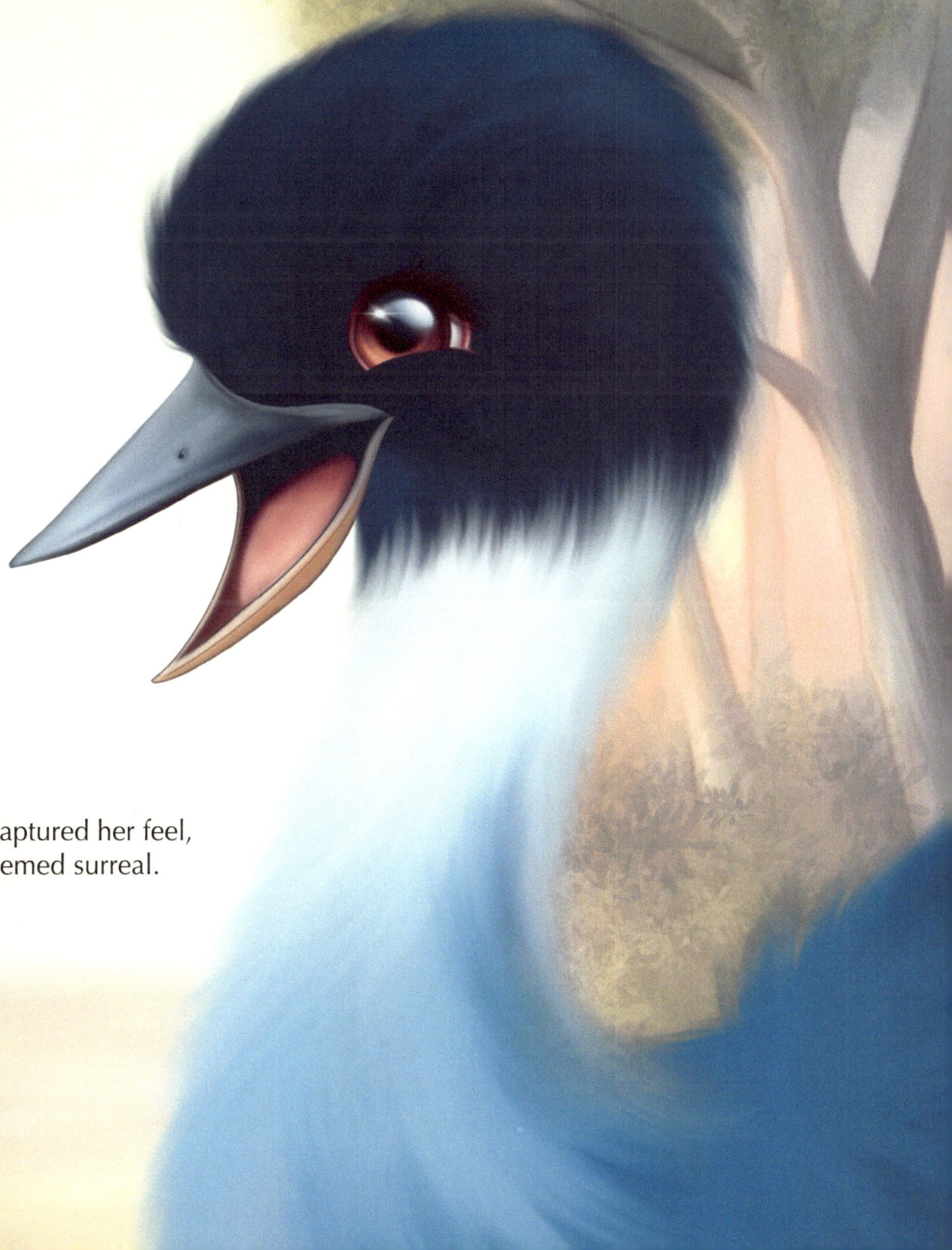

At last, the word that captured her feel,
  A joy so bright, it seemed surreal.

Esmeralda danced and pranced, repeating with cheer,
All the words from her friends so dear.

ECSTATIC

EMOTIONAL

EUPHORIC

EXHILARATED

But 'Elated' was the word that truly resonated.

And so, with a heart full of delight,
Esmeralda the Emu felt perfectly right.

Elated she was, and her joy she'd share,
With all her bush friends, everywhere.

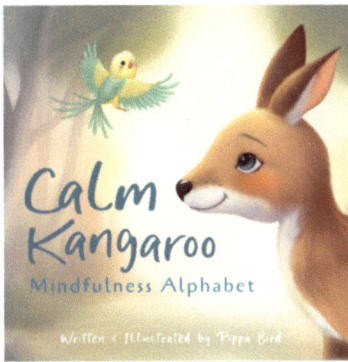
Calm Kangaroo
Mindfulness Alphabet
Written & Illustrated by Pippa Bird

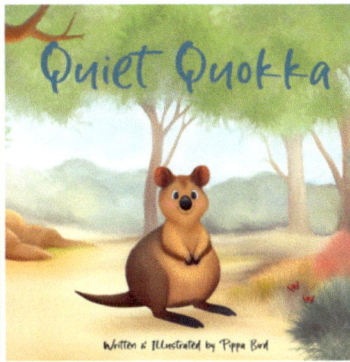
Quiet Quokka
Written & Illustrated by Pippa Bird

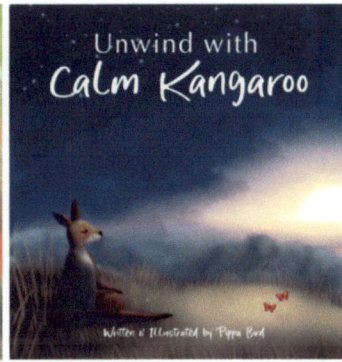
Unwind with Calm Kangaroo
Written & Illustrated by Pippa Bird

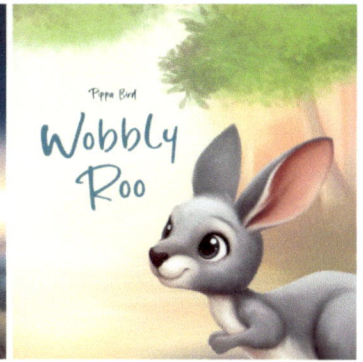
Pippa Bird
Wobbly Roo

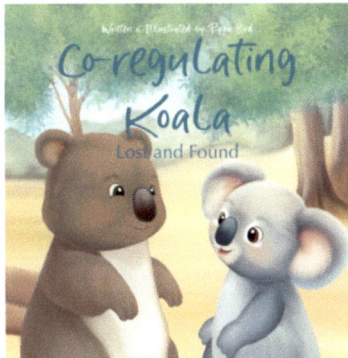
Written & Illustrated by Pippa Bird
Co-regulating Koala
Lost and Found

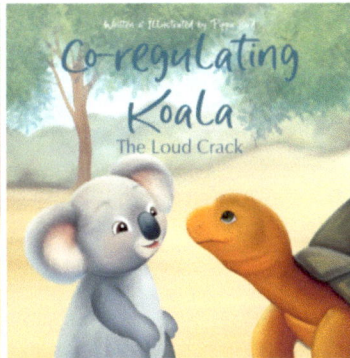
Written & Illustrated by Pippa Bird
Co-regulating Koala
The Loud Crack

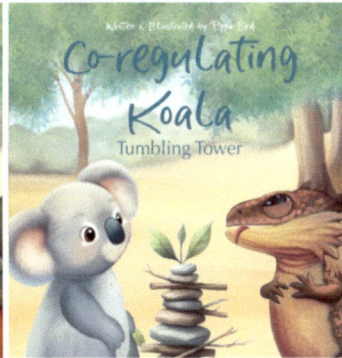
Written & Illustrated by Pippa Bird
Co-regulating Koala
Tumbling Tower

Logical Lyrebird
Pippa Bird

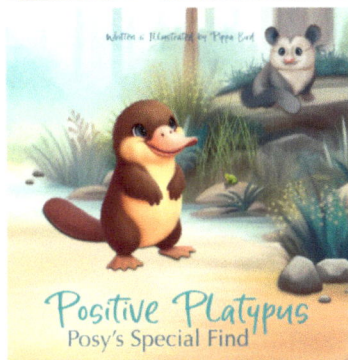
Written & Illustrated by Pippa Bird
Positive Platypus
Positive Platypus
Posy's Special Find

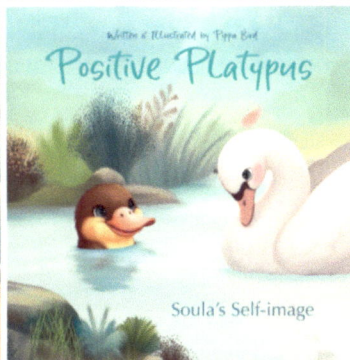
Written & Illustrated by Pippa Bird
Positive Platypus
Soula's Self-image

More from this series.

Introducing Calm Kangaroo's Mindfulness & Wellbeing Journal: 10 Week Program

Designed to enhance emotional learning and mental wellbeing. This delightful adventure invites children to explore mindfulness and self-care with weekly wellbeing check-ins and self-reflections, mindfulness colouring and expressive art activities. Available now on Amazon!

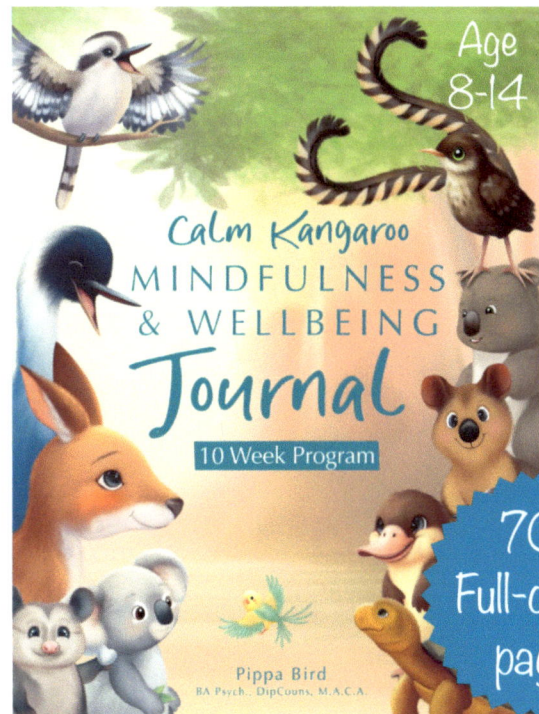
Age 8-14
Calm Kangaroo
MINDFULNESS & WELLBEING
Journal
10 Week Program
Pippa Bird
BA Psych., DipCouns, M.A.C.A.

70+ Full-colour pages

www.ingramcontent.com/pod-product-compliance
Lightning Source LLC
LaVergne TN
LVHW072125070426
835511LV00003B/91